Nancy

moment from
Plymouth to the
promised
land

now

JK Lawson
2014

John K Lawson was born in Birmingham in 1962. He emigrated to the USA in 1987 and became well known as a visual artist with work in many private and public collections. In the summer of 2005, whilst living in New Orleans he lost his home and studio to Hurricane Katrina, along with 25 years of artwork and writing. This is reflected in his 2007 novel *Hurricane Hotel*, and in some of the poems in *now*, his first full poetry collection. John is currently living on the Rame Peninsula, Cornwall, with the wind and the rain.

By the same author

Hurricane Hotel – a novel, Trafford Publishing 2007 (US)

Figures in Jazz – poems & artworks, Honfleur Ltd. 2013 (US)

Acknowledgements

Some of these poems have previously appeared in *The Berkshire Edge*.

Front cover image: *This is Not A Love Song* by JK Lawson.
Salvaged flood damaged map of New Orleans, encaustic, ink.
2008, 36" x 36" x 4". Collection of James Tegeder.

Foreword by David Woolley

In the early 1980s I was young and the world seemed full of possibilities. Abandoning a career in Law, I set out in the footsteps of Sal Paradise, Kerouac's hero from *On the Road*, to find life beyond the boundaries of the city of Plymouth. Several years of travel and itinerant working followed, with periods back home working and saving for the next trip. During one of these a football injury led to weeks on crutches, & I attended an Arvon Foundation Creative Writing Course, where my life was changed forever. I fell in thrall to the magic of modern poetry. From then on, my life seemed to be leading me on one course – that I had to make my living in some way from literature. This led me, in the mid-1980s, to start sending poems to literary magazines, and soon after to start my own magazine – a quarterly of poetry, short prose and artwork, *Westwords*.

Anyone who has anything to do with editing poetry magazines or running poetry competitions will tell you that you get sent an awful lot of rubbish. With all due respect, there are a lot of people out there who think they are touched by poetic genius, and most of them are misguided. It was therefore a great joy when submissions from good writers came in, even more so when they seemed to be new young writers, names never heard of. One day, I started to open a bulky overstuffed envelope, addressed in a spidery scrawl. Not promising. Neither was the burst of fag-ash that exited the envelope with a tumble of paper. But what was on those sheets of paper – wow – that was something else. I could feel immediately a real, original voice in the vibrant, quirky poems I read, and see a talent in the impossibly thin line drawings that came with them. Here, surely, was an exciting new discovery. I replied straight away, accepting both some poems and drawings, Seeing that the sender lived at nearby Tavistock I also suggested a meeting with this mysterious 'JK Lawson'.

The meeting soon took place, and was instantly the beginning of a short, intense friendship. JK – John Lawson – is a force of nature, and not to be resisted. Back then, we were young and stupid, and didn't have a clue what we were doing. In those pre-www, pre-social media days we were so much less in touch with the wider world, and what we did we had to discover for ourselves. In a frenzy of activity we wrote poetry, set up readings, set up workshops, bullied booksellers and generally went crazy. John was already then embarked on his dual creative process, and hassling anyone interested – paying off his bar-tabs with paintings, and trying to get his work seen. The indomitable Francis Mallett of the New Street Gallery on Plymouth's Barbican, took a risk on John, and gave him his first solo shows. But England then never really seemed quite big enough, or quite ready, for JK Lawson, and it wasn't long before John set off for the USA. As swiftly as he had blazed into my life, JK was gone from it.

No email then, and we soon lost touch. I went my own way, continuing *Westwords* as both magazine and poetry press, having my own first poetry collection published, and setting off for Cardiff University to study for a much-belated degree. From there, a career if it can be called that, in literature, dawned, taking in Essex and then back to Wales to work on Swansea's '1994 UK Year of Literature' – the world's biggest ever celebration of the word. I was supposed to go there for 18 months, but, as its most famous son Dylan Thomas said 'I got off the bus, and forgot to get back on again...' After the year, I was offered a year's contract to run the arts events at the newly opened Dylan Thomas Centre, then the annual Thomas festival too, and one year became three, became 15.

One sleepless night in 2008, I lay wondering what had become of JKL. I googled him, discovered his website, and found that he'd become a pretty big deal as an artist in the States. I also discovered that he'd been living in New Orleans and been blown away by Hurricane Katrina and the subsequent flooding. He had lost his house, and much of 20 years work, and only narrowly managed to save himself and his wife and young child. I emailed the address on the site and returned to bed. The next day I had a reply, and in frantic exchanges learned that John had just published a novel about his time in New Orleans – *Hurricane Hotel*. More amazingly, the 'novel for voices' had been heavily influenced by Dylan Thomas! As well as the novel, John had created a series of extraordinary collages, made from dried out pieces of artwork and writings recovered from his flooded home.

That summer John and his family came over. I arranged an exhibition of the remaining collages – like most of John's work, they had sold well – and a reading from the novel at the Dylan Thomas Centre. So we met again, after 20 years, and seamlessly took up where we had left off, both of us little changed, our friendship and mutual enthusiasm undimmed. John returned to the USA, and shortly after my life hit a rocky patch. I finally got back on the bus and left Swansea, but JK and I kept in touch intermittently via email.

By early 2014 my life had come full-circle, and I was now back living near Plymouth, just a few miles from where I'd been when I first knew John. In early summer I received an email to say that John was coming home to bury his father, and would be visiting his old haunts for a few days. John had an epiphany the moment he stepped off the plane in June 2014. His difficult relationship with his father had been one of the reasons he had fled the UK. Now his father was dead John knew that he could come home.

A few days in the south-west convinced him even more that this was where he belonged. Not so easy though, with a wife and son safely ensconced in New England, and still haunted by the ghost of Katrina. My new partner, Ann Gray, is also a poet, and the two got on instantly. We both realised that John was right, and that he could only fulfill his destiny by coming home. In typical JK style he had, within days, set up a studio and representation via Francis and Paul Somerville, and returned in September to begin a residency at the artists' colony at Maker in SE Cornwall. John came bearing his manuscript of poems, and within days had persuaded me to resuscitate *Westwords* as both poetry press and magazine, and begin with publishing his life's work!

And so we launched this book of poems, in partnership with Paul Somerville's Maker Gallery, surrounded by the artworks John had been creating during his residency. I'm pleased to say that the qualities I first saw in John's poetry a quarter of a century ago are still there, and with much more besides. In all those years in the USA

John has made his living, and a considerable reputation, as a visual artist. Apart from his novel, and the jazz poems accompanying his artwork in the beautiful book *Figures in Jazz,* John has published very little poetry in the USA and none in Britain since I published his poems in *Westwords* all those years ago. It is well beyond high time then that these remarkable poems should finally surface, having survived not only the passage of time, but also both hurricane and flood. So – what to say about this collection of poems?

Like all great artists, John Lawson is unique, yet his list of progenitors is long and strong. It starts with Whitman – this may seem odd, as John's line is mostly so short, whereas Walt's was mostly so long, but these lines sing. Dylan Thomas too, in that word-lust, that driving rhythm. Jack and the Beats of course, in the picaresque love of life, and especially Ginsberg – these poems howl with rage at the Great American Dream turned Nightmare. Lawson, like other clear echoes – John Steinbeck, Cormac McCarthy, Bruce Springsteen – is a champion of the down-trodden and the dispossessed, of the African Americans in their prison cells and the white-trash in their trucks by the thousand. JK is also the bard of the bar-room and the open road, echoing both Bob Dylan and Tom Waits, with his drunken bar-flys and his weary waitresses. Then there's the Southern Gothic element – Faulkner, Flannery O'Connor, *Deliverance.* There's more than a touch too of Raymond Carver, the great minimalist storyteller. A bunch of these poems are every bit as visceral, as affecting, as Altman's 'Short Cuts'. WS Merwin of course, in the abandonment of punctuation, relying instinctively instead on the living, driving pulse of true language, the heart-beat of pumping syntax and the natural pause of the line and stanza break. JK's influences are mostly American, and after half a lifetime there he has the idiom to a tee, yet added to that an element of wry English detachment comes into play. As a visual artist, you would expect these poems to be visual, but more than that they are wonderfully filmic. Many of these poems are like verse-versions of Coen Brothers movies!

We had some arguments JK & I about the centralising of the text, but he was right. Laying the poems out – and open – in this way adds to that immensely powerful, irresistible, torrent of language, the cumulative effect of which takes Lawson's poetry into another dimension. It's streamofconsciousness alright, but these poems are fully conscious of what they are doing and where they're going. Lawson's language, his rhythms, his skill as narrator, his powerful list of characters, his painter's eye for detail, his raw and truthful source material, are all always under control, especially in that hardest of hard places for the poet – the end. Time after time, we're seduced into the poem by the title, the striking first line, the whacky simile or crazy metaphor, but JK knows just how to end a poem. Powerful, musical, vivid, touching, angry, funny, profound – what more could anyone want from poems?

I think that's enough from me. It's time you went away and entered the world of JK Lawson – *now* – a rich yet often desperate world, one so full of wonder that we all must wonder, as John does here, just exactly why we've driven that world where we have – to the edge of the cliff. And that's where these beautiful, extraordinary, unique poems leave us now – see-sawing on the edge of our own stupidity, almost done, but still with perhaps a little breath, a sweet breath, of hope.

I can only finish by saying that I am absolutely delighted to be publishing this collection, by both an old friend and a new friend, but, as importantly, by someone with very special talents. The word genius is much over-used, but John's work, both his painting AND his poetry, are touched by it – undoubtedly, JK Lawson IS the real deal.

For my final words, I'll use the last lines of the poem I wrote when I heard what had happened to John during and after Katrina, and give grateful thanks to the fates that my words sang true:

and we'll surely be meeting up again and

you'll be blowing like you always were

just like a hurricane

David Woolley
Westwords Poetry
Autumn 2014

j k lawson

now

westwords poetry

First published in Great Britain in 2014 by Westwords
Publications, Coombe House, Lamellion, Liskeard, PL14 4JU

www.westwordspoetry.co.uk

ISBN 978 0 9513258 1 0

Printed and bound in Great Britain by TJ International Ltd,
Padstow

for Sebastian
may your sun always shine

"How much further can a blind man see?"

from *Hurricane Hotel* by J K Lawson

Contents

now

i am here and this is now

i am here and this is now
a land filled with everything
and containing nothing

a land swimming in bullets
and drowning in denial

i am here and this is how
watching the traffic grind to a halt
with engines running
with air conditioners running
and everyone and everything
running out for more

i am here and this is me
watching the weekenders
drive into their weekend town
in their expensive newly realized quasi organic cars
eager to buy their organic fruit and vegetables
at the local organic farmers market
with their organic farm bumper stickers
with organic sun tan lotion
smeared on their organic peeling plastic faces
staining their organically made clothes
washed in organic soap
made in not so organic places
by slaves to this oh so organic machine

i am here and this is how
organic churches and synagogues
fill up with organic children
with their organic toys and prayers
and organic puppies wagging their organic tails
at their masters slurping organic ice cream
before driving back to their organic homes

to watch organic shows
on how to do organic exercises
and cook their organic produce
so they can outlive their own organic lives
before driving in their expensive cars
to take an organic hike
on an organic mountain
or organically relaxing
in their organic gardens
filled with organic flowers
before getting back into their expensive new cars
to drive back into the organic town
to eat organic pizza and more organic ice cream
and sip organic tea before getting back
into their expensive new cars
to drive back to their expensive organic homes
to retire early to bed after checking their stocks
so they can sleep with organic dreams
and wake refreshed and organic
to do their organic exercises and meditations
before driving in their new expensive cars
with the radio talking about
bombs and bloody children
and saber tooth muslims
annihilating civilization
before making it back to their offices
and squash clubs
to play with themselves
figuring out another way
to decimate and gamble away
our non organic future

i am here and this is how
before and after the idea of work
can ever become realized

i am here and this is how
everything and everybody owning nothing
shuffle along without anybody else noticing

nothing is gaining ground
faster than the next high speed connection
with songs and chants and images of yet more bloody black men

i am here and here is nothing
except borders and prisons and guards and lawyers
and people paid to listen to nothing
except the tears and fears and crying mothers
complaining about having nothing
concealed and readily available
at the push of a button or pay as you go phone

i am here and now is nothing
like it was one minute ago
when the coffee was hot
and the dog feel asleep

i am here and this is nothing more than
another poem written out of a need to dream
of nothing reaching past the rejection slips
and tired reminders from family members
to get a real job and invest in the future
even though they see very little good
coming out of my future
it is better than me doing nothing

i am here and this is now
a time when anything is possible
for those smart enough not to wait
for someone to give them everything
without as much as a thank you
for having given them nothing

i am here and this is nothing
and this is nothing
and this nothing
can be
absolutely everything

i raise my glass to the perpetual error of self

i raise my glass to the perpetual error of self
bound by my love for decay
knowing little salvation can be found to cure these thoughts
i meander along the levee past the dispersing crowds
riddled in wave noise in search of a strangers hand

a chemical taste follows my footprints
sinking quicker than i can stand in the mississippi mud
the river reflects
a closed toy store with taped up windows
and dust covered treasure no longer for sale
except online

crawling up the muddy banks
a moon of glucose shimmers overhead
im lost again beside a blister of abandoned housing projects
confronting all hope claiming no hope
having learned early on
promises smell bad
and impulses furrow the brow

i am forced to accept that this flat world
full of ghosts and bullet holes
impatiently waits
to be flattened some more
before abstract faith reconciles
with the undiluted
dimension of time

barefoot dogs

living in sunshine louisiana
just before the dawn
a committee of voices
rioting inside my head

i roll over and feed the cat
old age seems to be winning
swaying and barely anchored
i make my way to the bottom
pilings of the mississippi bridge
and begin to climb

the peeling lead paint
the brittle iron splinters
cut my bare feet

sunglasses mirror the river below
on the fifth beam up i fight the belief
i need more air

a stranger joins me
his throat crackles methylated symbols
his clothes appear cleaner than mine
turns out he has been living beside
the bridge more years than he can count

what are you doing up here he croaks
i was thinking about jumping i say

what you going to hold onto when you fall

the wings of broken angels i shout
a glimpse at forgotten gods

we sit together on a rusting cross beam

im a poet
i proclaim

no he says
youre drunk

its air i need i protest
you wont find much down there he laughs

the rising sun shatters on fast moving ripples
a tug boats engine echoes across the levee

listen up he says your heart only hurts
from the inside out it passes
just stick around
after a while yall be able to tell the difference
between the rattling of rolling box cars
and rolling box cars rattling

maybe youre the poet around here
i say

minutes pass
we watch a pair of snapping turtles
basking below on the mud
you got anything to drink
he finally asks
back at the house i say
he carefully stands up
and makes his way down
off the bridge
i follow him and almost slip

cutting up across the damp fields
the melting dew glistens
looking back our footsteps resemble
a procession of swaggering forgotten gods

when ellie goes out cruising

three trailers down
wearing her granddaughters
cotton printed dress
ellies radiating with energy again

her body could be mistaken for 18
her mind is nowhere to be seen
armed with a pack of newports
and a bottle of fizzy lime water
she never makes it further than
the toll booth at exit 14

you see for the past three months
when ellie goes out cruising
she forgets to bring her beaded purse
drivers license and money

its become a routine
at the toll booth
a designated driver
tows her car off the on ramp
then carefully buckles her back
into the drivers seat

hoping like the rest of us
shes going to make it home
before her drunk ex husband
notices shes gone

hot snow

i was living in the ghetto
on chimes street baton rouge
when an explosion shook the building

later on that day we discovered part of exxon refinery
had simply given up refining

for a while we stood shivering half naked
on the broken balcony watching
as if in slow motion
glowing cancerous flakes
floating through the air

some of the flakes landed
on a nearby hyacinth bush
others on tops of cars

with your camera clicking
you said its all so surreal
like hot snow or something

i went inside
rolled a joint and tried to make gas masks
from a pile of dirty laundry

eventually you came back in

youd better take a shower i said
hiding underneath the covers
i was going to do that anyway you said
its christmas eve remember
and we have to go meet my folks at church

the withdrawal

empty bottles break
and the cold tonnage of steel
slides into a grey dockland sea

holding onto life
as if it were a dearly departed friend
questions often end up as quotations
scratched on the walls and forgotten
long before any answer is found

today in this square and breathless room
im waiting for the rain to stop repeating itself

the sketch i made
of a stick figure
resting his or her chin
on his or her knees
seems to have grown tired
watching the smoke
curl up to the ceiling

not wishing to escape
or start over again
i try and see what the windows reflect

fully aware
stillness and empty bottles
can only result
in too much thought
for the girl next door
questioning the quotations
found in a book of reflections
designed to enlighten
and disperse the terror
before one of us picks up
and cuts their fingers
on the shards of broken glass

now

now i have
the right to know
now the sun
has left me shadows

now i could
forget the bed
i spent last night
fighting in

now i refuse
stolen secrets

now i respect
what guilt can do
running uphill
to catch the bus

now im no longer hiding
the frown on my brow
feels easy

now i can direct my attention
to what ive always wanted

now the bee has stung me
i feel for the dying bees

now my ears
hear the songs
in falling leaves
i understand
winters silence

now i no longer think
about what to do next
or what next might happen

now im on a journey
i no longer need a knife
to open old wounds

now i accept my kingdom
is taped together
with paint paper and glue

now the noise of excuses
seems to make matters worse

now i can recycle
everything ive learned

now ive abandoned
my fathers calling
the idea of making a home
sounds less appealing

now i own the ability
to record my actions

now staring at a blank canvas
i feel the need for completion

now i can stop crawling
into every book ive read

now ive forgotten how
to start all over again

i can cry
when i watch you
trying so hard
to die

now talent is less important
than what can be accomplished
now the game
remains the same
i recognize there are no
winners or losers

now doing my best
almost feels normal

now i have learned
how to stumble
standing still

now garlic lingers
underneath my fingernails

now when paint
patterns my skin
flowerpots and stick cactus
seem less important

now i kiss my family
before they sleep and dream

and the way i grill salmon
has become a standard

now i write
instead of praying

and every day
begins with prayer

now im comforted
with footprints
entering a lake

now i can end
without a beginning

now i know
we all have to die
knowing now its pointless
to ask anyone
why

cave man

dry leaves twist and turn
falling from a molten sky
together again you talk
naturally with your hands
about dancing movement
and the shadows of puppets

resembling a looney tune
i mumble about connections
lassoing us to higher dimensions
aware my nerves are connecting
to the notion
memories of yesterdays
tonight feel real

you laugh saying my wires
are permanently crossed
from riding too close
to the everlasting flame
knowing the candles on the mantle
adore your naked frame

centuries ago
i would have dragged you
deep into a forbidden cave
before making you immortal
with blood soot and sweat

now given the odds
youre not going to stay
ill take what i can get
maybe drink a little less
cross my fingers
behind my back
and promise to behave

the sun resurrects my shadow

the sun resurrects my shadow
from melancholys silent dream
damp footprints disturb the rainbows
reflecting in distant streams

on drying boards and fences
apocalyptic birds
screech out your name
covering my ears is useless
standing in the thundering rain

being my usual clumsy self
tripping over empty bottles and cans
you told me once
death is a permanent vacation

and life without pain
a curious assemblage
of body parts
when mixed together
end up a collection of permanent stains

lucky night

if im lucky tonight
i might wake up
before its all over
before too soon
becomes the last dance

if im lucky tonight
as i stare at her thighs
i can catch myself dreaming
about bare back rides
through silver swamps
brushing palmetto leaves
as the wings of birds
rise above my face
into a sky
painted with rain

before promises are made
and desire is forgotten
with a little luck
i can fix the flat
and avoid the rats
watching the bugs
spinning around
bare bulb lights

ill forget the bruises
if im lucky tonight
and rips in my jeans
wrestling with snakes
hogging the jukebox
in the back of this barroom

if im lucky tonight
she wont mind too much

my floor being littered
with discarded clothes
and torn up paper
stained with
torn up words

with a little luck
there will be
enough gas in my truck
to drive her home
to sleep with the scars
falling from a sky
scorched by the moon

advice while texting

ive tried everything to expel
the demons prattling like bones
banging on a tar drum

and when i finally get a break
or find a moments silence

theres the monkeys next door
scratching on my back

have you tried meditation
she asks in a text

meditation
masturbation
constipation
contamination
free thinking frustration
every ation known to man

i see she says
but i can tell
she hasnt heard a word

they chase me
through the streets
on crowded subways
at bus stops
always on the news
underneath the bed

who do

the voices

they are relentless
and will stop at nothing
to drive me crazy

look around she says
well worship demi gods
with every new brand of tea
stretch before during and after
a longer work week
ban the obvious
only to have it replaced
with the less obvious
whiten our teeth
until they blind us in traffic
expel christ from christmas
make lists from the lists
digitalize friendship
design robots to kill our enemies
so we dont have to look
into their childrens eyes

in fact
we will do almost anything
except laugh at the joke
and accept our weakness
of all being stuck here
and briefly glued together

god youre so smart i say
no longer caring about her texting

not really she smiles
youre simply not listening hard enough
to the voices rattling inside your head

wake me

wake me
so i can
step into
another
faceless street
littered
with
self denial

stab me
watching
chalk drawn
borders
divide
the money
spent
in classrooms
on
crack
and
3d
printers

smoke me
way
beyond
my means
as i
tattoo
my
fist
on
trending
political
schemes

paint me
choking
knowing
we
borrow
from
the
dead
before
repaying
the next
holocaust

fine me
standing
in traffic
with a broken
dog bark
or holding
a
kitten
abandoned

see me
mimicking
lost
dreams
reflecting
in
a frightened
childs
smile

spinning inwards

spinning inwards pieces of ourselves seem
to fall apart each day
where they go no one knows perhaps theyre heaped
into a pile marked lost and forgotten perhaps theyre sucked
up as an invisible energy source radiating later through our eyes
fixed on blue tooth screams

either way she says i doubt if anyone hears them fall
or picks them up to use again later

we continue sipping our coffee
from the look on everyones face
tom waits isnt working this morning
its all so confusing she continues
we are rapidly becoming
clocks without hands
taking every mistake to mean
something more than personal

she starts playing with her tea spoon
he nods in agreement already
sensing shes tired of his little joke
about being sweet enough
thank you very much
every time a cute waitress
asks if he takes sugar

vincent

every time
he stares at the mirror
he sees her bathe dress
and exit the room
containing a beauty
beyond his control

today is no exception

the flesh of fresh paint
weeps onto his boots

he brushes his hair
takes a hit from a pipe
then runs down the stairs
into the busy misplaced streets

his mind is stuffed with tulips
dreaming of daffodils

with a razor in one hand
a bloody ear in the other
he has to see her again

disposable youth

jonesing after hours
back and forth through endless doors
finger tips resemble sandpaper
scratched over broken glass

in these times when the words runs out
its back to the bar for another round of abuse

as i brood contaminated with self a young man
recently back from iraq
dressed in silver spray painted combat boots
scrubs the stalls and cum stained bathroom walls

watching him toil
for all my wants and self inflicted needs
i feel a sense of luck stab me in the chest
sure im dumb enough to be fooled
in an hour or two
ill be swimming in a drug induced nirvana
no doubt im running from life with a pair of scissors
a screaming adult with childish problems
too far gone to reassemble the necessary parts
needed to break free
from a pre ordained zombie youth

always lusting it seems
to escape into tattoo ink and pale skin
wearing on my chest a handmade button
i graduated from the school of hard knocks

y all

perhaps without words caring for me
in the bartenders half crooked all knowing mind
i too might resemble something disposable
like an out dated childrens toy
or a stuffed panda
missing an eye
or the above mentioned boy
stoned and broken
wearing silver spray painted boots
scrubbing the bowls after another thrown away war

january

you have departed
now i know the reason why
on every footprint path
the snowman has to melt

chem trails

chem trails
criss cross
over the bells
chiming throughout
christendom

below a burning star
with itchy red eyes
if im not mistaken
theres a two headed bunny
desirously bobbing around
before shitting blood
on my neighbors glowing lawn

needless to say
i have to accept
denial is a deep river
and theres little chance
this poem will make
a public library shelf

inside the asylum

inside the asylum
of remembered thoughts
reason has no room for empathy
storm flies resemble fingerprints
textured moths twist
on floorboard dust
wings singed in the candles light

logs sliced thrown onto the fire
wallow in ash with never to finish poems
and this child charged song
scribbled to you
my sister of long distance dreams
sometimes like mine torn and tattered
locked in puzzles and endless corridors
and never ever
in technicolor

inside the asylum
of remembered thoughts
i write with a mind
stuffed with cheap wine
hammering on the keys
as if they were nails
hammering on the keys
as if sealing a coffin
passing each sentence
over the bare bulb light
blown in the roaming
ink tipped wind

hammering on a day
when sacrifices
cover my bed sheets

the bloody remains
of birds
shrews
and chipmunk brains
brought out of the dampness
by a wandering cat
a sign of her
loving affection
i am told to believe

hammering on the keys
to make it all different

hammering on the keys
to touch the distance
to unlock the door
and lead me out
into the eye spy images
of a childhood past

inside this asylum
words open up
like a dust covered book
removed from a shelf
marked lost and forgotten
remembering the days
when we skipped out of school
to dance through fields
laced with primrose and promise

hammering the keys
beside broken bottle neck creeks
and chestnut hollows
when apple blossom sailed
in the wild rose winds

hammering the keys
in search of fairy tales
wading through streams
deeper than the nile
dressed hand in hand
in hand me downs
singing made up songs
with magpies and swallows
swooping and diving
in the graveyards yawn

hammering the keys
remembering we cut our wrists
to become blood brothers
inscribing our youth
under a buckling cherry tree
too afraid to go home
and tell our parents
unable to step away from
the hidden rabbit traps

hammering the keys
as we encouraged
the circling crows
by feeding the crows
leftover dreams
until moving to a city
laced in pin pricked suits
where graffiti was studied
and stars were forgotten
running with a gang
with the most scars
discovering blood
in the backseat of a car
before the rule of fist

chained my wrists
to endless lists
and the beginning of this
now passing
child charged song

usual suspects

in various shapes and forms
the usual set of suspects
are lined up at the bar

its monday morning
and every one of us
feels safe with a room
a shared bathroom
knowing we are out
of the daily pain
of trying to produce

away from the sun
breathing stale air
we sit like snails
without our shells
in the cheapest hotel
on the prettiest avenue
in new orleans

over there
beside a clock
missing its hands
can of worms ted
a past life craw fisherman
nestles into a bar stool cavity
resembling a slaughtered chicken
sitting on an egg

his natural instinct
lights a camel non filter
and watches smoky question marks
curl up past the bets hes lost
galloping inside his head

two bar stools down
surrounded by ash trays
and vacant room keys
waiting to happen tuesday
pops a couple of pills
in between uncontrollable tears

shes been fighting again
because most of last night
fred did wednesday

after a brief stint
in the condemned bathroom
fred and tuesday
kiss and make up
choking on the news
scotty is d o a

the shock of his death
overcame us all
as we each recalled
only hours before
he sat at the bar
sipping his beer
with a pack of smokes
and a few bumps of coke
pissed off with the rest of us
the saints
werent going anywhere close
to winning the super bowl

he could have at least
lived long enough
to give me the rent check
tuesday says

uncrossing her legs
to reveal a set of fingers
loaded with rings
pointing in my direction

like you pay rent
fred mumbles

tuesday
downs her drink
and stares at me
yr good for twenty
aint you

i guess so i say

we stumble up stairs

if your gonna write
about me someday
she says
taking off her wig
quit being so fancy
and tell em
the fuckin truth

beating heart

take my beating heart
made with paper words and glue
hang it up for the shrink wrapped world
to air dry and view
pick it apart
poke it up close
then auction it off
for an exorbitant cost
only promise me one thing
you wont tell me where
my beating heart goes

some will ummm
some will ahhh
some will have a good laugh

but if youre really interested
ive started another
one of a kind piece
this time its an ear
actually
van goghs
precisely
taken from a bloody
photograph

rubbermaids

the rubbermaids are playing
at the hi ho lounge tonight
stumbling out of the drizzle
into an oasis of christmas lights
my eyes flicker on and off
in the candles flame

the poison ive swallowed earlier
helps me regain focus
helps the snakes in my veins
bite a little deeper

someone i once knew
throws a glass across into the air
im in no condition to fight
before the crash breaks loose
so i slump into a chair

the rubbermaids are playing
at the hi ho lounge tonight
in a heap the girl next to me
has already figured me out
as long as i dont vomit
or pee in her lap she says
theres a chance i might make it
out of here alive

i try to explain
earlier in the evening
my credit card was stolen
i drawl thinking im smiling
imaging a thiefs disappointment

the rubbermaids are playing
in the hi ho lounge tonight

the slithering in my veins
has now moved to my stomach
perhaps adding more to the mix
can reverse this never ending fix

im lost in a new world
sketching on napkins
cigarettes floating
in a pint glass of gin

the rubermaids are playing
in the hi ho lounge tonight
i offer the girl twenty bucks
if she can drive me home
she tells me i can crash
outside her front door
if i guess her name

lulu i say

the amount of loose change
stuffed in my jean pocket
equals my commitment
to try and behave

i like lulu she says
and hands me her lipstick
now go write a poem
on the bathroom mirror wall

the rubbermaids are playing
at the hi ho lounge tonight
on the mirror
in the bathroom
i write

lulu
makes me feel
real enough
to fondle the future
with a bottle of wine
and a lipstick kiss

the rubbermaids are playing
in the hi ho lounge tonight
youre a boneless wonder
lulu says
placing her lipstick
back in her bag

im seeking salvation
i slur in a laced up world
filled with endless possibilities
stray bullets
and muddy pearls

the rubbermaids have stopped playing
in the hi ho lounge tonight
lulu and her lipstick
have packed up and long gone
leaving me alone with a soggy napkin
knowing full well
whats going to happen
when the ambulance arrives
now ive finished off
my last line

the tattoo of touch

overflowing with past tomorrows
the glass you hold begs to be me
entangled in whispers
after chasing melting snowmen
i watch through the lace curtains
my prisoner combing her hair

nailed above the door
framed in burnt magnolia leaves
a pair of figurines wrestle with a lamp lit face

its times like these
before the first conversation
when two heartbeats are no longer strangers
i fail to accept there is no cure
to heal the tattoo of touch

only when i say so

you once told me
true love is sharing
the same dream
at the same time
like the night we submerged
underneath the magnolia trees

i was a junkie
zoo fish egg
then and now
you an intricate clock
wanting intimacy
yet tightly overwound

later that evening
after the party
a cop busted you
for reckless driving
you reminded me
as you were cuffed
to keep on lying
no matter how
it all went down

in the back seat
of the squad car
you cried as the cop
drove 85 mph
all the way down
river road

i followed
in his tail
driving your car
smashed
without a license

six hours later
when you were released
i drove us back to your apartment
thanks for lying you said
youre welcome i replied
can we fuck now

looking back at it all
i have to laugh
two weeks later
you threw me out

youre a lying cheat you said
i thought that was okay i said
only when i say so you said

today
i received your note
telling me how
we were never real lovers
merely a pair of misguided
wanted ads
photo collaged
on the same back page
with apartments for rent
kittens for sale
lawns to be mowed

waking up
in the bed of this truck
watching the fog lift
revealing a bunch of birds
with webbed feet
and long curling beaks
overturning tiny shells
in the low tide
i have to agree

leaves sound like keys scratching across the street

lightening nears and the wind picks up
brown magnolia leaves sound like keys
scratching across the empty streets
tiny tim found shelter
with a band of cockroaches
sitting on an awning covered stoop
sirens wail
church bells ring
a stranger walks up and offers him
a swig from a pint bottle
wrapped in a brown paper bag
have you ever he says in the
galloping rain tilted your head back
with your dry mouth wide open and
wondered what its like to drown

i cant say i have tiny tim replies
you will someday chuckles the stranger sitting on the stoop
sipping the pint they watch the rain
tiny tim notices hes wearing a pair of muck boots
heavy overalls and owns the hands of a farmer
what do you do for a job
i take care of the ponies working the buggies
thats cool
not really i smell of horse manure all day an night
it takes me forever to clean up the pays good though
trouble is i gotta check myself for mushrooms every day
they finish the bottle
whys that tiny tim asks
to make sure none of them are growing on me
tiny tim laughs a tad giddy from the cheap booze
i thought mushrooms only grow in cow shit
cow shit horse shit dog shit
you aint going to tell me no mushroom knows no difference
you do have a point tiny tim says

the stranger doesnt hear him
hes already walking off into the wind
watching the lightening and brown magnolia leaves
sound like keys scratching across the street

one for the mice

squeak squeak
is hardly the way to begin a poem
and yet the mice underneath my bed
running up and down the walls
seem to be egging me on

they seem content
with the pacing and thumping
cussing and door slamming
followed with days of silence
as i sit around waiting
for the next right thing
to magically happen
and the next disaster
to disappear

knowing you probably
have already forgotten
what you said about my poems
knowing you will never forget
what you said about my behavior

if i stop now
im a goner

i figured this ones for the mice
living in the plaster
hanging out under the floor boards
partying with the fleas and neighbors

i have to respect them
theyre survivors
not in the least bit concerned
if the power goes out
or the a c breaks down

or the bloody blisters
flaking loose skin
from my swollen feet
from running away
from a pair of drunken thugs
last week
on bourbon street
will ever heal

squeak squeak
a few more
and ill be squeaking along
with these bastards

telling them
how someday
ill have it all

telling them
in my own mice like language
how living by the ocean
with mermaids
rolling in the waves
sipping mango fuelled juices
with rainbow umbrellas
sticking out of tall iced glasses
is so much better
than remembering
the way your naked body
deranged the night

lullaby in a minefield

there are devils grinning
inside the silence
a great longing
to be with the engines
burning through the blue vapor
criss crossing the sky
spraying who knows what
into our childrens classrooms

my mind is a lullaby in a minefield
out there with the continual reminders
of self improvement
and positive vibrations
glued onto broken
bits of images

and flayed over
barbed wire fences
blood shot deserts
and sunny college
campus parking lots

staying busy
in a city choked with phlegm
i can ignore and diet
free associate
with my inner being
chase the chant
bend and stretch
believe the fable
love once said
if you reach the mountain top
a face will appear radiating
and when you have seen the face
the body and fingers will be easy

your mind will be comforted
in what was never seen before
and all things after this
shall be different
complete
safe
and your future
shall have no end

so i lit a cigarette
blew a fuse too many
and took a chance
off a third floor balcony
only to land
headfirst
back into the devils silence

frenchie

its a bad habit he cant live without
inspecting his reflection
impatiently waiting
for a head
or two
to roll

behind a layer of grime and shower curtain floral
he scratches flakes of dried expression
from his wrinkled skin

today hes on a quest
for nonstop happiness

after all the room is paid for
the cats out of the bag
pearl jam is jamming
and hes sold a couple of paintings

the smell of the complementary
all purpose body wash
inspires memories of a lost girlfriends
late mother

standing in a pool of water
he clenches his fists and challenges the sink

tighten your belly
butter bean
learn to express
the expense
after all
theres very little
to chew on
except ourselves

the streets have grown ears and black eyes

a world without
twists into
the world within

streets have grown
ears and black eyes
watching the blood
feed the sewers of discontent

everyday
every hour
on the hour
a colony
of sub consciousness
falls asleep

looking forward
seems to begin with
looking
whos covering
my back

thankfully
i follow the moon
and no longer
have to stand and stare
in front of mirrors
my soul is with the poets
who believe

if this is whats left
within and without
the universe
can perceive truth

thankfully
i follow the ocean
and hear the waves whispering
in the smiles of friends
scribbling on walls
and writing their own futures
saying

its time to stop the sink
from clogging

a game of chance

this wobbly table
this radiator fuming
these two cracked
snowman glasses
this spilt red wine
this make shift bed
this bag of used tricks
this bouquet of roses
this shaking fist
this derelict smile
this book of matches
this blood pounding heart
this mess on your dress
this smell of your flesh
this taste on my lips
this pillow of chop sticks
this stain on the carpet
this raging hard on
this can of dog food
this greasy pot
this assortment of spoons
these bites on my neck
this broken clock
this hammer and toothbrush
this squashed mosquito on the wall
this pile of torn clothing
this hot wax and ice cube
this left open fridge
this rope and scarf
these scratch marks on my back
this corner of empties
this head filled with holes
this devoured box of chocolates

all appear to be playing
a game of chance
with the fires
burning inside
your eyes

lost in a void

below the balcony
past the buzz
of the frozen wires
adrift on a crumbling planet
spun off its own axis
he watches his unarmed lover
foot stepping home

breath choking her face
a heart cuffed with stars
lost in a void
of unreasonable space
smoke becomes curtains
curtains become smoke

in another room
a kettle brings to boil
whats left of the day
to a childhood memory
following a milkman
as he made his early morning rounds

coffee made
made coffee

remembering now
to rummage through a drawer
filled with takeout menus
chop sticks coins and spent keys

slipping his wedding ring
back on his finger
before showering
last night away

one string guitar henry

one string guitar henry
shuffles his sores from limb to limb
his blistered lips mumble
blistered tunes to mother melpomene

hustling along the cracked tracks of
oretha castle haleys boulevard
he remembers way back when one string songs
made a couple of hits in the malt liquor bars
south of north rampart street

silent now the diabetes has kicked in he enters
the mission with three overcoats
worn over a flower painted shirt

he takes a seat knowing full well
hell be the first to confess
hes been born again
as many times
as hes been lost and found

isolation is the best cure for loneliness

sometimes it seems
isolation is the best cure for loneliness
waking after a recurring nightmare
staged behind a piano
with too many broken keys
foggy memories haunt him
from the night before

he vaguely remembers trying to exit
the scene rather like one of those indian muskrats
he saw on tv they can crawl along 20ft tunnels in search
of python eggs the tunnels are so narrow the animal
has no way of turning around
and is unprotected should the python return

the cold shower does very little to
calm his nerves he does however find comfort
knowing whatever might have happened
has nothing to do with the rising cost of postage
stamps and how in his college days
mailing bricks wrapped in newsprint seemed radical

dressed now
nothing appears to be broken
his phone remains to be found but there are a few
hard boiled eggs sitting in the fridge

a parade of faces passes

a parade of faces passes
revealing artificial feelings in the annual
trick of treating twisted skulls
pre formed bones and made in china
adult romper suits

everyone it seems is trying
to conceal the brutality of facts

three flights down the fire lit torches
cast warped shadows
over the ghosts of our former selves
who appear busy and ant like
texting new possibilities

and wouldnt you know it
all at once
at the very same time
i am forced to accept in this seamless
age of dry wall conscience
bound by plastic mementoes
naked inked pimps
and scum bag bankers
my compulsion to hide and hoard
has little effect on saving the arctic whale
or polar bear or the mindless sea of gutter punks
smashed on daiquiris and hand grenades
determined to break down
my neighbors bullet addled door

kelly

wearing a pair of soft white cotton socks
last night kelly won another round of dead mans bluff
it was the usual set up
he was at home on the rocks
self absorbed and writing
speckled patterns drifted over the scars
stained in lost miles
kelly was out having fun with her work mates
and reluctantly stumbled home simply
because she had an early shift the next day

stripping off her clothes she said
why do you write so many poems
about love
and stay so unhappy
they arent love poems he sulked
sure theyre not
she laughed slowly walking past him before
sitting on the couch rolling a joint and turning on the tv

images of children covered in flies flashed on the screen
bored she picked up a sheet of crumpled paper
and between hits studied his words scrawled on the page
well she said at last
if this isnt trying to be a love poem i dont know what is
what does it say
you really want to know
yes i do
she stood up gestured a bow and read

note to self
comma
we chart our destiny
with the mangled stars
scratched on subway glass

sometimez

sometimez
the day goes like this
wobbly on my bike again
out of tune
with the traffics buzz
risking life and limb
and the overworked cabbie
avoiding the bewildered
flock of tourists
before colliding
into a shyster banker
or a nanny clutching
six shiny babies
and a party set
of birthday balloons

sometimez
i feel like a clown
missing his clown suit
a hacked up wordsmith
peddling his wares
over man made man traps
avoiding pot holes
both real and imaginary
half filled with zombies
crossing the dotted lines
at various speeds
with various skills
talking on cell phones
dialled into nowhere

thankfully
i have my faults
to cling onto
and a broken horn

that squeaks
instead of honks
and a few simple words
constantly jumbled
up and down
this way and that
searching for
the perfect way to describe
the details
found beneath
your flowering cotton skirt

islander

above the hullabaloo
with a map of cornwall
pasted to my chest
ive been up all night
absorbing the blue

listening to angels
dance with the rain
in broken gutters
and sewers flooded
with forgotten brains

there is no doubt
this storm understands
my madness
connects the dots
and washes away
any pretense
to remain calm

washes away my chains
long before the alarm clocks buzz
next door and down the hall
where men among men
snore and roar
with their broken lives
their hunched shoulders
and sore knees
wrapped in winter silks

to make matters worse
on a piece of paper i scrawl
a map with buried treasure
and a note that reads

someone
someday
will take your hand
petal delicate
and hold you beyond
a mere mans swagger

i pin the words to the wall
knowing left to my own devices
im on the verge of emerging
as an uncrowned king
returning from a voyage
amazed at his kingdom of towels
bathrobes hotel toiletries
confiscated letters and parking tickets

amazed how they all seem
to have their own special place
in his broken suitcase
with its peculiar stains and burn marks

and how after all these years
they remain important enough
never to close the suitcase
to stay dry and part of the energy needed
to keep me writing and not think about you
sleeping alone or with some pathetic moron

the cat licks her paws
hot coffee mixes with smoke

a quick sketch of tomorrow
makes the impossible appear a little closer
makes me want you to join me again
and in my mind complete a sentence
before setting sail

makes me real enough to dive a little deeper
and save the paper scraps from the water
dribbling now from the buckled ceiling

makes me honest enough
to jump out of the window
dressed in my well used bathrobe
and sit on the wet rooftop
to claim my waterlogged kingdom
underneath the fire escape
and broken umbrella

knowing i can bask
in the rain
in beer can bliss
knowing i am
and always will be
an islander
at heart

some guy upstairs

there he is again
some guy upstairs
before leaving his room
every morning
i can hear him
spitting on his shoes
muttering about
how he mistrusts
being human

the other day
he brought a frog
into the barroom
and dared anyone
to swallow it whole

he didnt offer anything
in return for the dare

the frog sat
underneath a pint glass
in the middle of the bar

people came and drank
the frog was ignored

finally
stan took out his buck knife
picked up the pint glass
and pinned the frog to the bar top

the frog didnt blink
as its back legs twitched
for a minute or two
then it died

as you would expect
someone suggested
the dead frog
might taste good fried

strange with freedom i shall roam

strange
with freedom
i shall roam
before the stars
lose control and fall
onto screens
·etched in odorless colors
and 50 odd channels
fusing a wayward vision

strange
with freedom
i shall roam
because today i am
brave enough to say
i can shed
my fold away skin
and break down
the gate keepers door
unlocking a journey
leading me through
a maze of pollutants
and hidden chambers
laced in vacant faces

strange
with freedom
i shall roam
past the blistered skin
of a crying white night

throwing my keys
into the itching sewers
never looking back
to scratch the bowls

plagued with sales
and forget me knots
held in clenched fists
disguised as open hands

past the commerce
of regulated birth
past disposable deserts
lacking sand and salt
past peeling walls
hiding unbelievable dreams

for i have heard
the vultures laugh
at those who search
for visible hearts
to beat against
the granite slabs
beneath the trappings
of what has passed
beneath the buzzing
of buckled street lights
where textured moths
and termites gather
forming clouds
before they dive
into the flickering
and buzzing
street lights

strange
with freedom
i shall roam
through rusting fields
over grown with rusted cars

i will roll my soul
into a shapeless dough
touching unknowns
no longer caring
if my nakedness
can be clothed

for i have heard
the vultures laugh
and am unafraid
if this approaching storm
jokes and curses
my silent labor
filled with unknowns
and seeking cures

strange
with freedom
i shall roam
before the one eyed moon
decides to blink
before a last kiss
has taken effect
to sabotage my heart
with what has become
a drop of blood spilt
from an ocean of veins
resting in a crevice
large enough to hold
long lost demons
now crackling and boiling
over this promised land
this paper peeling view
i once called home

waiting at your door

rusting pink flamingos litter the lawn
a bag of old clothes is hidden in weeds
overflowing onto the busted curb
clumps of dead flowers are strange reminders of balding scalps
its jazz fest season and amidst the crowds and confusion
im knocking on your door

storm clouds are circling within and around me
a distant gunshot becomes a scream
my life consists of rooting for loose change
earlier i ate two eggs over easy with burnt toast
now my stomach wants something more
im almost out of smokes
banging my head on your door

last night i dreamed of avocado bellies
thigh tattoos and my hands running through
your curly brown hair
today the streets have bent me out of shape
a neighbor is yelling cut the god damn grass
i slide on my knees then crash on your stoop
waiting for you
to open your door

night has come and gone
i didnt sleep or take a sip
unable to hold your smile in my mind
the decaying stars twinkle a little less
and appear further away
ive got to go to work within the hour
but have a feeling im not going anywhere today

ive named the broken flamingos
the colors of the rainbow
someones started cutting the grass next door

the garbage has been picked up
and its started to rain
other than that little else has changed
waiting for you
to open the door

things are getting weird again

things are getting weird again
theres raindrops dripping
inside my head
i am trying to write
fallen silk touches the stars
changing the shapes of shadows
but have no idea what any of it means

i do know we came here
perfect and open
only to end up as collapsible
deck chairs
marooned on a muddy beach
unable to shrug off
post victorian values
across the world wide web
of spreadsheet words
slogans and disputable facts

where maps replace letters
and fingers raw thumbs
carefully cracked
then tacked
onto movable office walls
creating cell like ears
to track and recreate
prisons of our own designs

yes things are getting weird again
after all
i have evolved into monitoring
my screams
and
left alone to my own desires
i have the immense capability to

fuck up my worst nightmares
however simple and predictable
until all thats left
becomes a numb display of passion
punched on ever reducing keypads
signaling a final rush
to break free again
and learn to feel

living miracle

everyone knows honesty
is the best form of medicine

two days later
when he finally came around
strapped to a gurney
in the emergency ward of charity hospital

the examining doctor
in front of fifteen
medical students
pronounced him
a living miracle

i dont feel like one he said

the blood tests
the doctor continued
identify half a dozen
known narcotic substances
moving through
your over worked
blood stream

tell you the truth he replied
i can only remember two of them

old glory

old glory is covered in a noon day sweat

his television flickers richter abstractions

he dangles his toes in a plastic pool

its good for his hemorrhoids
or so hes been told

his forest of nose hair twitches
from the neighbors garbage

a cloud of fruit flies hover
over his beer stained breath

children across the street
play in bare feet
on hand made skateboards

whooping and hollering
cussing up a storm

back and forth they go

if only i had me
one of them aka 47 s

old glory yells

just think how much quieter
this neighborhood would be

empty pockets

the craving for flesh
has started again
washed away words
mix with delusions
weaving thru flashes of lights
and a chorus of horns blowing

im back in a city
living close to the streets
i can barely afford
with hardly enough excuses
to pay for this rain soaked ride

aware nothing can wash away
the reflection of her smile
mirrored in every puddle
i stubble into

velvet bar rooms
laced in fresh vice
empty my pockets
until driven deeper
into underground corridors
where obscene billboards
clash with homeless reality

sneers appear
peering over the financial times
gawking at the obscure poor
beleaguered and damned

forcing me to crawl
into a deafening silence
and finish the ride
in a state of denial

back here
in the broom swept cave
collaging her face
into a pile of returned
postdated rent checks
i pull a few lost words
from the smoke choked air
and begin to sketch the floor

focusing on the details
in an attempt to capture
traces of her lipstick
on shards of broken glass

road trip

im only going to say this once
he kept repeating to himself

im only going to say this once
before the drugs wear off

lets make it happen
lets start a new beginning

bone on bone
go for it

as if we were two wild beasts
alone in the park

let the layers peel free
above the noise of rattling subways

leave everything behind
wash our hands

scrub our nails
and tear ourselves to bits

until all thats left
is raw nerves and guts

like the rabbit we found
trapped in a barbed wire fence

on a blistering day
when a road trip to dalton

ended up
in a ditch somewhere

everything will work out

its kind of sad
you once wrote like that she said

handing me a water logged notebook
fished from a collapsed book case

perhaps everything will work out
for you after all

perhaps i said
adjusting the mask straps
tangled in her hair

you know i said
its funny you should say that

say what

i think i wrote something along those lines
several years ago

oh yeah she said

watching me remove my disposable gloves
and start flipping through the wet pages

found it i said

sloshing knee deep
in contaminated flood water
i walked towards the light of the window

is it as bad as all the rest she said

i pretended not to listen
and began to read aloud

perhaps everything will work out
after all
there hasnt been a cop in popeyes
parking lot for the last two hours
perhaps everything will work out
if only i could quit worrying about the cockroach
no longer twitching beside my last line

youre really sick she said
taking my notebook
and stuffing it into a garbage bag

i guess so i said
walking into the kitchen

honey
what now
lets not deal with the fridge today

connecting misplaced dots

there are days when connecting
misplaced dots seems easy
the sun appears to be round
and im happy to say if it stays in the sky
instead of burning my eyes
i can remember to smile
at the packs of roaming dogs
following me from street to street

all these drawling dogs
who seem to say
he seems harmless enough
well devour him another day
give him a break
make him think its all easy
make him feel hes wanted
a happy slice of a sticky cake

let him get back to his own business
pacing without direction
with images of destroyed cities
and water supplies being cut off
to thousands of americans

let he
who really cares
scorch his mind

because sooner than later
hes going to understand
one thing
in order to survive
vast doses of daily abandonment
have to be administered
to numb the slap on the face reminders

this all for one nonsense
is going to the garbage dump
regardless of ring tones

let him have to wake up
and recognize the minutes
have caught up with the hours
and the seconds
now mimic entire scripts
distorting reality
into convincing
self sustainability
is really a package unwrapped
and forever comfortable with a shitty lot
settling and useless

like a yard of wet dirt
and yes we all know there are days
when he really ties to imagine a world
filled with love and joy
a world that can carry you and me
and all of us together
just as the wind carries this newspaper
he finally stopped reading

and yes he is one of those poets
with hands always working
long after his head has been chopped off

and yes he dreams in such confusion
connecting displaced dots
wanting to join the first
second and third worlds
into one big collective finger
giving corporate greed the bird

but we all know
left to his own devices
well be eating him alive
just as the weekend evolves into
another over scheduled work day

chuck

chucks been sleeping
in the back yard again

pa dont seem to mind
as long as he dont mess
with his chickens

bolan at the hardware store
says last week he went and brought
a brand new axe

one of those fifty pounders
and hes been sharpening it ever since

just in case i run out of razors chuck told him

well i dont like it or him ma barks
heez goin need more than a weed whacker
to get that crows nest off his face

oh quit yr frettin ma says pa
the worst hes goin do is chop down
a white house or two
and use it for kindling

lucy sounds nice

lucy sounds nice made her bed and smiled
everything had started to become manageable
after the motor bike accident left half her face on the gravel road
she felt for the first time in her young adult life
a sense of freedom

no more snide remarks from the other girls at school
no more teachers wanting her to stay after class
no more daddy staying home at night drunk groping and playing daddy
it was as if she had evolved into a glowing tibetan rock
you know like the ones in the tie dye stores
and everything she now focused on could become real

with the insurance money
training to be a nurse instead of a model was an option
maybe one day write a short poem
nothing too fancy mind you
just a simple poem
something about a snowman sitting in the sun

wrinkle

i watch you slap your grandchild around
in the museum of modern man
all the child said was
what is this stuff
wheres the sound
and why isnt anybody laughing

given the chance id follow you home
rig your lawnmower to explode
before your watery eyes
and let the birds peck at your shriveled
bloody pieces

thankfully the grass does a better job
taking its sweet time
to return
day after day
blade after blade
to torture your cold blooded soul

slow motion

caught in a net
fished out by a rising dawn
the limp night sky fades
over the peeling rooftops

protecting the stacked sleepers
paying homage to a mother
kissing away the fear
on a childs cut finger

wiping the frost stained window
he spies a sparrow
unfolding her wings
displaying a bone structure
few men can achieve

confusing the snow flake air
as if filmed in slow motion
the tiny bird flies to the frozen ground
and starts pecking at the ice
until her beak is broken

the chase

headless leaf blowers
have joined forces
with the weed whackers
and are out there again
chasing me down
from lawn to lawn
parking lot to empty garage
cemetery to grave stone

with little chance of me
making it out unscathed

i am armed to the teeth
with an overflowing cup
of scolding shitty coffee
and forced to resort
to extreme measures
conjured up within
the dank corners
of my soul

a scheme
for sweet revenge
this too shall pass
becomes so old
i forget to repeat it
again and again

instead never fear
and take the bastards out
seems far more do able

given the creeping shadows
are holding all the cards

randall

trying to breathe inside
a pair of odd shoes
his swollen feet shuffle
sluggish footsteps
over another worn out mile

doughnuts dipped in
cold coffee
have their own sensibility he muses
and makes a mental note
to write this down

racing ahead
past last nights televised dreams
old screams seem to be winning again

yawning taxis belch past
polluting a cough mixture
no doctor can cure

waiting at the bus stop
he finds temporary distraction
listening to a pack of derelict men
with rusted voices
reminiscing over yesterdays
when jobs had value
and chicks with thighs
had a real set of tits

the shock of it all

on the tip of my burning tongue
the numbness into the mysterious
has been solved and life has found me again

rain clouds are forming
long awaited appointments
have been duly cancelled

ive caught up with myself
crawling into the corner
overwhelmed with so much truth

my hands are blistered
from tearing up roots
my lips in the mirror
resemble a burst balloon
the eggs i tried to fry
have turned into beer coasters
attracting a pack of flies

through the shock of it all
i did manage to remember
to fix the front lock
perhaps the landlord was right
ive been lost in too many
delusional day dreams
for far too long
and now its time to unravel
on someone elses dime

last night before she left
i was told very loudly
how i make her feel

stuffed into an airmail letter
she said
with insufficient postage
before being thrown into a sack
to be deposited in a deserted post office
with no chance of ever being delivered
and no return to sender address

thankfully the clown downstairs
distracts needless pain

hes cursing at the tourists again
complaining how hes not interested in their applause
its cash he needs
for the next ride out of here

i can relate to that
everywhere i go
smiling lunatics follow me
toothpaste becomes a luxury
my boots shrink in the mornings

and i must admit ive grown tired
almost to the point of exhaustion
trying to understand
in the middle of the day
why some folks feel its their right to say
they only drink to forget

ive seen what can happen after we die

its a crazy business
said the blind man
sitting on his stoop

but ive seen what can happen
after we die

the hearse runs out of gas
at a blinking red light
and twelve stretched out limousines
create a parade of sorts

backing up traffic
along st charles avenue

causing a scene
in the midday heat
the chauffeurs start to fight over
who is going to fill up
the red gas can

the children of the deceased
dressed in their sunday best
exit their cars
and start playing tag
in the medium

waving at the
passing streetcar tourists
and singing

look what can happen
after you die

spray painted gold

graffiti
sure im not gonna lie
and say i understand
what all the fuss is about

still not bad for a couple of days work

all in all given the price of the jack hammer
the motel room the generator
the extra pair of gloves the goggles
the meals out the fork lift the truck rental
the crow bars the sledge hammer
and the gas to and fro
its a pretty penny im forecasting

sure the store keeper next door
wasnt a happy camper
but mention those two magical words
green card
and bingo
where did he go

seriously its like what i kept telling
those tv reporters
who really cares

certainly not anyone
in this trashed out neighborhood

least im doing something constructive
least im investing
in my own future

watching flowers grow out of the gutters

watching flowers grow out of the gutters
in a world at times too dangerous
to undress my mind
leaves me leaving one place
in some unexpected hurry
only to find the next place
smells the same

writing
taking 20 minutes to walk one mile
ss the speed i last left you
doesnt help to justify
my impulse to leap
out of this rented tomb

now im learning how to become
a one lump or two
kind of guy

knowing there is never enough pain
to undo my favorite mistakes

and follow through without listening
to old men with frustrated desires
mumbling about all the things
i shouldnt do

they complain about the time
i waste writing
fantasizing about the next time
i might get laid
as they rummage
through garage sales
collecting change
in nickel and dime stores

i on the other hand
ignore their remarks
run from their red noses
and continue on my quest
painting footprints in the snow

they and who are they anyway
seem to have forgotten
i have found a purpose in life
dancing in the shadows
on a quest for more light

at night when i ask sleep
to wrap her arms in velvet desire
i count naked women
wearing cowboy boots
instead of sheep

sure the strawberries i brought
are now rotting in the fridge
yet im always ready
for the next feast
the next knock on the door
the next lucky break
watching flowers grow
out of the gutters
in the rain

small talk

midafternoon
sipping
watching without too much

thinking about all the great poems
i will someday write
in a fancy notebook
instead of this napkin

the front door opens

shadows choke in the sunlight

jay staggers in
with his beer can gig
and broken jaw

hes a legend
scrawled on many
a bathroom wall

you wanna drink
i say hoping hell say no

spare me yr loose change
jay drawls

how come yr in such a good mood
i say chomping on the ice

last night i won me
3 rounds of russian roulette jay grins
pointing to a wad of cash
crammed down his front pocket

hey now you can buy the beer i grin back
moving a little closer

fuck yr small talk
unless you want to walk the walk
jay mumbles

before passing out
on a broken bar stool

dollars for daze

do you ever wonder she said
after they had finished
with the usual slew of introductions
what might happen in the next sixty seconds
we count pennies
like minutes and dollars for days
a week could be an ancient time piece or a
shopping cart filled with tin cans
months become loans stuffed with high interest
and the inevitable years a collection of keys
or a cool quote from a dead poet
tattooed on your arm

we collect pennies in mason jars
and the numb chance of a
lotto ticket becomes our only weekend highlight
and so it goes on as another bomb drops
as a new day sells out with the roar of car
alarms and drive by shootings noticed by no one

what do you suggest i do about it he said
giving her his concerned smile moving closer
realizing this was not going to be easy
she laughed you can start by flossing
the spinach out of your teeth

going clean

im keeping my shit
together this time
all the misery
and self destruction
is being neatly tucked away
out of harms way
in a jean pocket
next to my rusting zipper

sowing up the seams
of all my ill intentions
with pins and needles
stitched to cushions
and rag dolls
web covered angels
and beads

the ones
too obvious to hide
im going to disguise
with cool t shirts
mirror sun glasses
and sock puppets
when i can find them

going clean
exiting the party
i was never invited
to attend

avoiding so called friends
who wait for me to join
davy joness locker
or worse
find religion

giving up my seat
on the back of the next bus home
too knackered to argue about
nails and broken glass
words and bullets
suppressing the obvious

its time to
bleach out the stains
rediscover whitman
keats and browning

disconnect the bats
flying inside my head
hot wire the nerves
to laugh at the funnies
turn a light on the shadows
chasing me across town

eat cereal

and discover
once and for all
what its like
to be normal

marcus

some folks are lucky
they are born on a different planet
some not so much
take my neighbor for example
across the hall

hes an artist

i do my best to avoid him
and ill tell you why

marcus sculpts his toe nails
with a carving knife
and electric grinder

one day he cornered me
at the bus stop

she haunts me he said
so i haunt her back

really i say
taking note of his footwear

she haunts me he repeats
but its never at night
never in the silent places
never in the eyes
of someone else

really i say again
searching for something new to look at

its at the gas station
filling up for a destination

or at the store
waiting in line for an under paid cashier
to ring me up

or worse
and this happens a lot
sitting in my kitchen
watching an egg boil

on a roll

shes sleeping tonight
beneath a bed of fire
keeping me awake
with a pack of matches

clouds the size of ants
roll over my eyes
my fingers are permanently stained
resembling chopsticks
broken in half

im stuck in limbo land
in a limbo land town

waiting for something to happen
in between closing and opening hours
determined to become
something i have already become

after all
i recently heard
from a high brow snobbish fellow
how in his opinion
i managed to waste twenty years of my life
writing a bunch of crap
not fit to be wiped on toilet paper

when i mentioned
i have used toilet paper to write
some of my best meditations on
the silence on the other end of the phone
was abruptly broken by my girl
punching me on the nose

needless to say i didnt get the job
nor laid for a week
but i did find a few new words to write
musing on the toilet seat
this poem being one of them

wheres rumi now

wheres rumi now
i for one could use a little help
to take one step backwards
and move my heartbeat forward

looking around if i am lucky
today could end up
a last minute tomorrow
captured under the fading
bare light bulb

i dress in obsolete fashion
and look for a place to eat

the waitress knows my sort
she takes a smoke break
before placing my order

can you tell me i ask
before the knife enters the pork
at what point does the noise
in my brain become a silent scream

i can tell youre not a tipper
she replies

i am too i say

baloney she growls
pouring me stale coffee
i know one damn thing

whats that i ask

your problem is the rawness
you say youre feeling and wear
like a preppy school boy badge

is because youre always trying
so hard to scratch
every available itch

rockin red rooster

the fog rolled over the levee
before settling around our truck
its like a fat ass nightmare
landed on my lap
you said

we were lost again
on river road
in a section of louisiana
called cancer alley

theres a neon beer sign i said
i think thats the rockin red rooster
we cant go in there
they will think youre a yankee
sure we can

we walk into a room filled with christmas lights

you havent been here before the bartender says
folks like you dont come down this far
unless theyre visiting the leper colony in carville
im researchin i say
bullshit he says youre drunk
that too i say
the room filled up with eyes
glaring in one direction
my girlfriend said you cut the heads off chickens here
we cut the heads off a lot of things its called making gumbo

for a couple of minutes no one spoke
the eyes became daggers
before returning to eyes
before returning to daggers again

wheres the nearest gas station

far from hope
the bartender replies

wheres that i say
sunshine he says
but we still call it for what it is
youre joking right
nope
they changed the name after the song came out
by the governor
no shit i say
theres no cussing in here says a pair of daggers

can i get a drink
that depends
depends on what
how fast you can drink it

i can drink pretty fast

he hands me a can of pabst blue ribbon
and a small plastic cup with ice
a dollar fifty

whats this i say
pointing to the cup half filled with ice

its called a to go cup
and dont expect no change

out from nowhere

a chorus of voices sings
regardless of consequences

tingling senses break
in the flames
i can breathe again

a new history is remembered
long before its rewritten

all the poet ever wants
is childhoods magic
to enter within

its time to look
into where we are ourselves

where we are going
depends on what we might become

armed with pen ink and impulses
a cosmic samurai
slices open
an egg
chains
locks and electronic screams

free imagination
roams and takes form
in the steam of a coffee cup
creating new songs
filled with echoes

daze go by
cures come and go
jumbled angst
sits on lazy hands

i option open smiles
to bloated stains
any day of the week

on the disheveled doorstep
on the corner of a misplaced block
tired shadows slip into futures laughter

energy
conversation
and perhaps once more
the shedding of our skins
reveals a sense of what is lost
can be found
in the power of new thoughts

ever so often
when the clock stops ticking
i think of candle wax
ice cubes
and your bare skin

multi tasking

multi tasking isnt as cracked up as it used to be
and i beg to differ women can do it better
aside from the near fatal car accidents while texting
less dramatic yet perhaps just as permanent damages
can happen in the domestic front

last night was no exception
the phone rang
i was in the middle of hot gluing
my new mantra onto the fridge
using recycled magnetized letters

poetry displaces
is as far as i got

as i reached for the phone
i knocked over a large bag of turmeric
the bag split and the phone continued to ring

i sat on the recently tiled kitchen floor
some guy a voice said
lou is that you i replied

before the voice had time to answer
i went on a tirade

when i was finished lou said
it could be worse the tiled floor could have been white
it was white i shouted
and aside from the potential benefits of curing alzheimers
lowering my cholesterol and providing me some cardiovascular
protection
no matter how much baking soda
bleach and steel wool i arduously apply
everything that was once white off white

made of wood tile cloth or metal is now stained
albeit aromatically
stale mustard

lou has the knack of making grave matters funny
and before long we were both bantering
about the good ole days

im getting used to the new mustard hue i said
it brings back fond memories of cigarette stained ceilings
and fingers and teeth
soap dish and shower stall
sheets pillowcases
plastic toilet seat sometimes
when it wasnt being used as an emergency flotation device often
knickers
speak for yourself
blinds ceiling fan blades
lamp shade when i was attempting domestic silliness
toilet paper
flannel

fell off the back of a truck painting apparently priceless
by the norwegian expressionist
edward munch entitled the scream

the dog you found on decatur street
for that matter
the gutter punk you found on decatur street
hey now for the record it found me
an original blue dog painting your dog peed on
now totally worthless

ooh back to nicotine stains
a jaded group of water vessels

probably early 18th century
in the form of two large joined open flowers
i had forgotten about them
a stuffed magpie
a 200 piece cut crystal chandelier
borrowed from an estate sale
too heavy to hang on the ceiling

buttons
burnt rubber duckys
worn out birth certificate lambeth hospital
cooked cocaine
tortured souls
a slew of fake id s
death certificate greenwich hospital

a chipped porcelain vase of the kangxi period
containing life savings condoms jack knifes
an lp box set of the entire magic roundabout
more buttons
ransom notes hand written and received
two unopened packs of glow in the dark stars
another dog who found you on the streets
pez dispenser
batman walkie talkie
barbie doll missing an arm
used rolling papers
little jimmy osmond lp
small stone gargoyle
what happened to the gargoyle by the way
g clamps rope various firearms
now stashed in an undisclosed location
five gallon sheet rock buckets
turned up on end and used as furniture
magnetized tiles glue gun newly trashed floor

lou says i gotta go now
i light a cigarette and write all this down
on stale mustard paper

muse

let it be said he said
i will find the colors
to paint your flowing body

and these lines
so delicately drawn
belong to an angels shadow

let it be said he said
your eyes

oh your eyes hold treasures
far beyond the waves
rolling on a forbidden shore

as for your smile
it leaves the canvas
begging for more

let it be said she said
i want
50 bucks an hour
and you can quit
the bullshit

gratitude isnt normal

somewhere deep inside
a tune is playing a farewell march
to another dumb war

today
sobriety is kicking my ass

earlier
i couldnt find my metro card

a punk dressed in a suit
half my age
yelled

get on with it old man

i kept my fists in my pockets
as a kind lady
swiped
her senior card for me

the chewing gum munching
bus driver nodded for me to move on

i sit at the back of the bus

seething and scheming
of all the things i want to do to the punk
now eyeing a cute girl

id start real slow
maybe with my elbow

no

id go straight for the throat
like the time outside the dungeon
when a couple of geezers
got the better of my mate
bouncer red

jumping in
i simply wouldnt let go
keeping my teeth
on an ear
till i hear a crunch

until the blood
began to flow

minutes pass

i realize as ive been
day dreaming

im staring at
a union sticker

welders do it
better
under gas light

in black marker
scrawled over the sticker
someone else has written

ha ha
no wonder

everyone
loves
electricity

i miss my exit
walk a few blocks in the rain

trying to remain grateful
simply isnt normal

the coffee shop is packed
with a clean set of beards

i keep my hands in my pockets
avoiding ear contact

piped in through speakers
the size of golf balls

a radio is playing
a farewell march
to another dumb war

positive thinking

lizzies dangling her half inked body
out of my bedroom window again

look at all those planets and stars
spinning madly around
somehow they manage
to avoid us she says

its the middle of the day i say
and youre three flights up
all i can see is burnt wires
a flock of pigeons shitting on cars
and two lucky dolphins
swimming on your ass

thats your problem she says
youve lost all your positive thinking
youre worse than a used up
four letter word

ill tell you where im at i yell
picturing the beauty of her mess
collapsing on my lap
and its not gazing into heaven

i let go of a leg
light her a cigarette
and start yelling again

im doing just fine
with my own set of positive thinking
thank you very much

just ask the quack down the hall
whos offering bucket rate scripts

for us lucky sods
stuck on the ground
doing the best we can
to avoid all your planets and stars
spinning around
messing with my future

war dogs

the dogs of war are at it again
biting for scraps
at the bottom of an oily barrel
ive given up reading the news she said
and taken up painting my nails deep purple
no more daily feeds or blogs for me
im going back in time and finding out
what got us into this mess

good luck i say
can you pass me the ketchup

there has to be a specific point
she continues
before the days of comparing
whose torture is better or worse
a time when chemically altering
our food with toxins
was considered biological warfare
or acts of terrorism

a specific date
when the lines of the unemployed
didnt end up incarcerated
or miraculously shrunk
wrapped into dollar stores
sprouting across our garbage strewn streets
turning whats left of the collective dream
into a white washed sarcastic scream

honey i say
this bacon tastes funny
and before you go any further
may i suggest
you stop taking
the kids to church

star

thats how it all got started

i followed him around from town to town
for about two years

then
he finally noticed me

he gave me a few pieces of broken string
as mementoes
and i havent looked back ever since

the pays not so great
to tell you the truth
i havent made a penny

but im an only child
and what they say about daddy spoiling me
is true you know

i wouldnt call myself a real artist
a performer yes

its amazing what can be done
with sock puppets these days

thank you

we could run out of excuses
faster than our drinking water

we could say all reminders are wasted
on the next set of super bowl commercials

we could write
the children across the street
running in bare feet
will someday grow up happy
and unafraid of the cops

we could pretend
there is a chance of catching a balloon
once the string has been released

we could say to each other
i undress my thoughts
as your thoughts
my failings
as your failings

thank you

we could believe
leaving one place releases another
while sitting on a borrowed wooden ladder
we could argue
there is no such thing
as justifying ones actions
if the impulse to die is dumb enough

we could demand every politician
spend a month in a morgue
before deciding on our future

we could raise the stakes to minimal
we could prove the foolish believes in repetition
we could dream there is always something better
if we recognize our own faults
and treat them as gifts

we could share common knowledge

we could ask our children to design their own schools
perhaps re evaluate the idea
all things that hurt are truths

we could say this will never happen again
is like saying a chained junk yard dog
will not eat meat

we could say desire
on all levels
is better than no desire
on any level

we could lie and say prevention is better than a cure
we could pretend the beginning started with creativity
and life is too precious for me to vote

we could learn a lot more from animals

i could start and end this poem
your feelings
are my feelings
your failings
my failings

thank you

gloria

gloria waves as the ferry
leaves the harbor

i like my faults she muses
even on sunny days
they give me pause
and something to think about

seagulls land on the table next to her

she opens a wrapper of tin foil
and begins to eat a thinly sliced
cheese and pickle sandwich

they are my special friends
she continues
i can carry them through empty crowds
and keep them secret

unlike these scars on my arms

they help me protect my inner smile
and fill the gap between
what ive seen and what i know now

and so it goes

loose memories of 4 am
and after
slipping up a flight of stairs
into an old barn
stacked high with furniture
and sticky white labels

stuck to covered sheets
with no bills of sale
no conditions of contract
just a silent gavel
and the curse of being unable
to knock a square peg
through another round hole

waking to the realization
found in a finger smeared glass
waiting for a few liquid thoughts
to drip then spill
before disappearing
into rotten coarse fabric

the side to side glance
followed by a footless crawl
outside to chase imaginary rainbows
beating against my chest

falling
into a snow covered field
then a frozen stream
hardly realized
as if id seen both
on a blue screen
or a different timeline
long before i cared to ask

what does this really mean
long before i dumbly waited
for an answer to lead me back
into my own set of rules
with my own blue screen
my own precious timeline

and so it goes

acknowledging
the drawn curtains
cannot hide
the furnace of sunlight
and all the cinders
the melting ice
the thawed footprints
the wishful songs
of birds and daily commerce
all moving along
in spite of their broken selves

all slogging and swaying
into the grey tear stare
of cubicles and tunnels
boxes and chairs
with hammers
and calculators
blank smiles
and incinerators
long ago forgotten
by the never ending winds
swallowing a few brittle leaves
blown in from nowhere

blood relatives

its the risk i have to take
when the living outnumber the dead

drinking in the c note
in an unlit section of town
standing next to the father of the son
my testimony just sent to prison

ive killed a man for less he says

what are you talking about i say
trying to figure out what i can hit him with
i have a gun in my pocket he says
look around i say so does everyone else in here

his wife returns from the bathroom
wiping her nose and twitching
youre not from around here she says
not anymore i say
what are you doing here anyways
good question
can i buy you both a drink
sure they say

we drink in silence
your son did try to rob me at gunpoint i say

hes pulled a gun and robbed me many a time
but i never called the cops on him the father replies

the drinks end

should i run now i say

not until you buy us another round
sounds fair to me

wrestling with the what ifs

im wrestling with all the what ifs
punching the rounds in my brain
every time i look in the mirror
i see the same bruised mistakes
knocking me back again
complicating my illusions

ive been handed a job to do in this life
and given the odds
none of it makes much sense
with a pencil and notepad and a slew of questions
piled up next to the shadows
constantly following me
across this weathered town
i have to find a cure

ive found me a room
without a view
so i can rewire my brain
yet all i can think about
is the trickling tickling sweat
running down your thighs
underneath the new dress
i brought from a market in santa fe
that lucky time when we watched the sky on fire
in the month of may
when the wind blew warmth
across the nape of our necks

you begged the driver to go a little faster
until the tire blew and the sirens
sobered us up enough
to hide in a motel where your dress
sure worked some magic
because shortly after

i found myself married
with a child well on its way

neither of us cared
love is cloaked in ruin
and spilt coffee stains the carpet

neither of us were expecting the glass
to be no longer half filled
with how can we make this work
even though you still make me hotter than hell
every time you slam the screen door in my face

the mayor of main street

he shuffles his limbs
from lamp post to lamp post
dog bone to dog bone
pushing his home in a shopping cart

armed with pen paper
and an assortment of hard candy
he spins his hours with tedious study
next to a radiator
in the public library

he could be
a spray painted prophet
or in my book
a collaged messiah
filling in the gaps
plugging up the holes
of our crumbling daze
symbolized as far out
or way too cool

moving into a thicker mass
past the condemned row houses
laced with crack
and broken promises
i follow this strange puppeteer
who it seems
prefers to let go of the strings
and the ability to connect
the hands and the heads
the legs and arms of instruction

choosing instead
to be homeless

regardless of season
or good fortune
content to dumpster dive
alone and without forgiveness

bobbing bottles

in a haphazard daze
having stumbled
through mountains of spent youth
and disasters
making more messes
than clean ups

guilty of groping
my way through
and over indulging in
all consumers spin offs

these jumping broken
blades of sunlight

trapped inside
empty bottles

bobbing in a sink

seem to say
this morning
is important enough
to question
what passing moment
will i miss the most

nothing left to own

now
theres nothing left to own
in this once bustling
worn out town
except these words
i scribble down
drawn and quartered
through listless streets
hollow bars
and messed up skirts
my mind burns alive
no matter how damaged
the gutters can feel

now
theres nothing left to own
in this rented womb
i call a room
another sleepless hour
might well prove
the rumors of freedom
bound in cages
and buzzed over screens
where animals are tamed
are absolutely untrue

now
theres nothing left to own
the fleeing cross
the belching blows
the throw away keep sakes
and abandoned kitchens
once decorated
in shades of sea foam
seem to haunt the daze

with x d out calendars
spent receipts
and lists of things
we can never undo

now
theres nothing left to own
in this sliced to bits
worn out town
three doors down
past the cats meow
two bodies submerge
in a bed of bullets
as if all that loves
is meant to bleed
over petty crimes
and phony receipts

myrtle

myrtle dreams of domestic genocide
overriding the common sense of the mundane
shes armed with a carving knife and meat tenderizer
ready to bust up the newly installed faux granite
kitchen island and sink

shes been known for a lot worse
once a dangerous example
for teeth whitening products
today with wire cutters in hand
its disconnect hour
starting with the dishwasher
then the oven
kettle and blender

shes itemized how to finish the job
and posted it on her fridge
with her husbands chainsaw
shes downsizing the vacuum cleaner
and divvying up the minivan

the letter her sister sent her
a few days earlier didnt help matters
all that talk about how in these troubled times
we should hold each others hand
reassure the young everything will be fine
learn how to magically let go
pray a little harder
work a little more
breathe a little deeper
and accept where we are
is really where we should be
regardless of dreams or desires

myrtle wasnt buying any of it
she rolled up the letter and fed it to the fire
now marvin gayes greatest hits
isnt happening anymore
a volcano has erupted inside her soul
grateful at forty for discovering ginger baker
and a license to bear arms
she is fully aware an ever gaping hole is swallowing her up
suffocating the next hair appointment
the next car pool thursday
the next u p s delivery

something somewhere somehow has to give
before the neighbors hear about it
before she showers and dresses
before her prescriptions run out
before the kids come home from school

this is not a love song

this is not a love song
crossing another time zone
only to realize
all clocks look the same

watching the sun
sprinkle diamonds
on the puddles of today

images of you
burn my eyes
never awake
long enough to sleep

remembering you once said
i dont care if you forget
to cross yr i s
and dot yr t s
just send me something
with a stamp on it

before i get up

another day
recoils into action
birds chirp
squirrels gnaw
dogs bark
cats meow
cows munch
hens peck
flies buzz
ice melts
bullets kill
bombs drop
police bully
politicians lie
bankers rob
drunks drink
children cry
fish fry
eggs break
fingertips burn
tea brews
coffee stains
cars brake
a cyclist wrecks
windows open
windows close
fans blow
fans suck
smokers cough
sirens wail

and my baby
turns on
the telly

silence cures no one

the absence of breath
hangs heavy in believing
silence is a cure
for lifes inflexibility

shadows have no wings
and yet
in the corner of disbelief
memory giggles

today
you taste like a watermelon popsicle
tomorrow
the stain on a printed cotton skirt
i recoil a little deeper
snake like self absorbed
in the present moment

shaped by my own folly
figures move
across the sketch pad

inked in
blotted out
then shaded
into life like proportions
mimicking what can be achieved

for some the world stays obscured
for others life resembles life
leaving the natural self to resurface
as the creator of another unfinished day
and stand without fear to capture

the hungry screaming crowds
beaten bloody with clubs labeled
protect and serve

a crowd whose only hope
turns into a mob
requiring so much more than these
fleeting impressions i paint

moving on

moving on
one room like any other
overturned dust
resettles on the top shelf

behind a makeshift desk
he finds empty bottles
an odd shoe
and a poem
sent from you

pinned on the wall
cheap postcards remind him
where you have been
and where
he needs to go

on the bed
covered with a sheet
often used
forever stained
he reads

time cannot heal
a broken clock

affirmations

theres days when i can relate to all the positive posts
affirmations quotes and sayings
when the birds singing outside seem to make sense
and being in nature doesnt completely terrify me
i feel like im really moving on
gaining ground on a slippery slope

im content the shakes have gone someplace else to sleep

my rented tomb has a door again

its true i havent made the big time writing a single line of poetry
and there are days when the granite steps of this library look
homely
but honestly if i wanted to be enlightened in any shape
or form i would have washed her tears off my fingertips
many moons ago

forgiving the odds

hurricane katrina hit
from new orleans we drove north east
this is easy you thought
this is the fat piece of the sticky cake

i paid 900 dollars a month to park my van
then waited in line at the red cross

with one gallon of white paint
your cousins apartment
became our make shift home

once you finally fell asleep
i paced without direction
images of a destroyed city
scorched on my mind

you wouldnt believe the mess
shoveled in our face

i wrote on the back of old photographs
where we are born
abandonment becomes part of the scenery
often disguised in the way we dress

years passed and now im reading about detroit
the bastards turned the water off

one city has too much
another not enough

perhaps theres a connection
perhaps thats what lifes struggle is all about
perhaps given the odds
trust and caring are really four letter words

used every four years
and hate and anger and greed
run this crap show
from the bottom feeders
on down

the other side of me

the other side of me
disconnects a phone
steps out of a room
stumbles down four flights of stairs
onto a frozen street

the other side of me
hails a cab
drops a bag at his feet
knowing his mission to nowhere
is nowhere near complete

the other side of me
cant decide if the pills or the bills
will beat him tonight
or join the other side of me
on the long road to silence

the cabbie turns on the radio
the rising price of oil
and anti smoking laws
seem to be connected
with smiling plastic faces
telling him to stay warm

the other side of me
feels the shivers kicking in
hears every word
in his skull
stop in mid sentence

at a red light
he jumps the fare and runs

no one stops him

beside a broken fountain
the other side of me
finds the movement of hungry pigeons
disturbing the snow covered gravel
vaguely interesting

on the back of his hand
in thick black marker
someone has written
its easier to dance
with two left feet
than stand alone
waiting

the other side of me
realizes he lives in a world of tin cans
and twist offs
and is paralyzed
with the beauty of textured moths
singed in the flames

underneath his coat
close to his heart
strange myths brew

if the ice age is really on its way
hes going to learn
a new sign language

the other side of me
notices cracks in the reservoir walls

he watches a man stop in his tracks
then stare at his army issued boots

in the brittle snow
he unties his laces
then staggers away in his socks

the other side of me
thinks
hes not a guru
with an unlit cigarette butt
protruding from his blistered mouth

maybe a poet

or an out of breath man
trying to retrace his past
as if this might be his last past
before the ticking of the clock
becomes too loud
and another bomb drops

the other side of me
wants to stretch a canvas
the size of poland
and paint snow in the snow
hes not sure why he chose poland
maybe its because
kafka was born there

maybe its because
he doesnt understand t g i f

the other side of me
isnt going home tonight
if his bathroom roof didnt leak
he could bawl out the landlord
even up the odds a little

rivers of veins are running dry
for the other side of me
the plastic bags
caught in leafless trees
remind him how
hes supposed to make a wish
every time he sees a shooting star

he doesnt bother
looking up at the sky
but makes a wish anyway

the other side of me
wishes this world
could grow up
and never grow old